Coloring Book

Improve Optimism and Positive Thinking

I0420386

Coloring Images with Mantras
Change Your Outlook and Perspective on Life

By Bella Stitt

INTRODUCTION

Feeling calm and relaxed creates an optimal time to receive and internalize positive messages that you, when stressed, are unable to process. For that reason, positive messages (mantras) are added above the symmetrical drawings in this coloring book.

Symmetrical images allow you to choose and use same colors on both right and left side of the drawing. While performing this balancing act, left and right sides of the pathways of your brain communicate with one another, binding emotional and logical thinking together.

Besides inducing balance in your thinking and feeling, coloring of symmetrical images creates a deeper form of relaxation and meditation. Your senses participate in this activity to further enhance your self-awareness and mindfulness. The balance of images captures your EYES. Your HANDS engage in the movement by the motion from left to right and up and down coloring. You are able to SMELL crayons or markers and can have a candle or calming oil infuse the air with appealing and relaxing smells. Your EARS are able to hear the sound of the color penetrating into the paper. In order to promote your sense of hearing, you can listen to music that will provoke feelings generally associated with arousal. In addition, to include your sense of TASTE in this activity, you can chew gum or have a hard candy in your mouth in order to absorb your sense of taste.

Combining both concentration and relaxation while introducing and continuously reinforcing a positive message is a great way to communicate with your conscious and subconscious mind, correct, and improve your inner voice and inner critic.

The coloring images in this book are simple and unique enough to allow you to almost mindlessly color while being in a hypnosis-like state to offset negative thinking and improve your confidence, perspective, self-love, self-worth and ability to experience joy and happiness in life.

Working with many clients who have depression and anxiety, I am more than aware of the damage that critical self-talk and pessimistic outlook on yourself and life can cause to your mental health and quality of life.

It is very important to overcome and counter negative thoughts and experiences with positive images and encouraging beliefs!

You can successfully correct and redirect your outlook into a positive frame of mind and state of being. This coloring book can help you do that.

What others say is a reflection of them, not you.

The only approval you need is your own.

I am strong because I know my weaknesses.

Be yourself. Everyone else is taken.

Attitude is everything. I got this!

It isn't who you are that holds you back; it's who you think you aren't.

I don't have to be perfect to be confident.

My attitude can permeate all external conditions.

Don't worry! Be happy!

I believe in myself. I'm excited about my talents, gifts, and qualities.

At the end of the day, what matters most is how you see yourself.

Fearlessly be your true self. You matter!

No one can make you feel unworthy without your permission.

Just because life is not perfect, does not mean that it is not wonderful.

I have the power to transform my life.

No pain. No gain!

I am beautiful because I am aware of my flaws.

I am responsible for creating happiness in my life.

I am perfect just as I am.

Just do it!

Accept everything you are — and aren't. That is true happiness.

I am wise because I learn from my mistakes.

I can do this. I have what it takes.

I am worthy of living my life the way I want to live.

I am capable of overcoming obstacles in my life.